SCHIRMER'S LIBRARY
OF MUSICAL CLASSICS

FRANZ SCHUBERT

SONGS

With Piano Accompaniment

English Translations by
DR. THEODORE BAKER

G. SCHIRMER, Inc.

DISTRIBUTED BY
HAL•LEONARD®
CORPORATION
7777 W. BLUEMOUND RD. P.O. BOX 13819 MILWAUKEE, WI 53213

CONTENTS.

The Erl-King.
(ERLKÖNIG.)

FR. SCHUBERT.

Who rides there so late through night so wild? A loving father with his young child; He clasp'd his boy close with his fond

Wer rei - tet so spät durch Nacht und Wind? Es ist der Va - ter mit sei - nem Kind; er hat den Kna - ben wohl in dem

6534

arm, And clos - er, closer to keep him warm.
Arm, er fasst ihn sicher, er hält ihn warm.

"Dear son, what makes thy sweet face grow so
„Mein Sohn, was birgst du so bang dein Ge-

white?" "See, fa - ther, 'tis the Erl - king in
sicht?" „Siehst, Va - ter, du den Erl - kö - nig

sight! The Erl - king stands there with crown and
nicht? Den Er - len - kö - nig mit Kron' und

shroud!" "Dear son, it is some mist-y cloud."
Schweif?" „Mein Sohn, es ist ein Ne - bel-streif."

"Thou dear - - est boy, wilt
„Du lie - - bes Kind, komm,

come with me? And man - - y
geh' mit mir! gar schö - ne

games I'll play_____ with thee; Where
Spie - le spiel'_____ ich mit dir; manch'

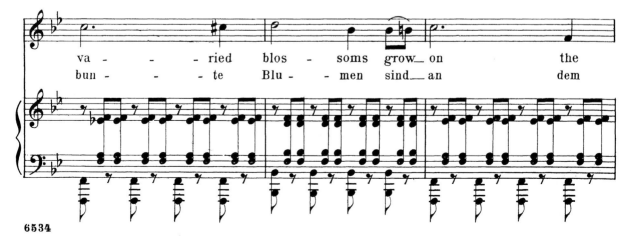

va - - ried blos - soms grow__ on the
bun - - te Blu - men sind__ an dem

wild."
Wind."

"Wilt come, proud boy, wilt thou come with me? Where my
„Willst, fei - ner Kna - be, du mit mir gehn? mei - ne

beau - teous daugh-ter doth wait for thee; With my daugh-ter thou'lt join in the
Töch - ter sol - len dich war - ten schön, mei - ne Töch - ter___ füh - ren den

dance ev-'ry night, She'll lull thee with sweet songs to give thee de-light, And
nächt - li-chen Reih'n und wie - gen und tan - zen und sin - gen dich ein, sie

lull thee with sweet songs to give thee de - light."
wie - gen und tan - zen und sin - gen dich ein."

"Dear fa - ther, my
„Mein Va - ter, mein

fa - ther, And can'st thou not trace The Erl-king's daughter in yon dark
Va - ter und siehst du nicht dort Erl - kö - nigs Töch-ter am dü - stern

place?" "Dear son, dear son, the
Ort?" „Mein Sohn, mein Sohn, ich

form you there see Is on - ly the hol - low grey wil - low
seh' es ge - nau, es schei - nen die al - ten Wei - den so

tree." "I
grau." „Ich

love thee well, with me thou shalt ride on my course, And if thou'rt un-
lie - be dich, mich reizt dei - ne schö - ne Ge - stalt; und bist du nicht

will - ing, I seize thee by force!" "Oh fa - ther! My
wil - lig, so brauch' ich Ge - walt." „Mein Va - ter, mein

fa - ther! thy child clos - er clasp, Erl - king hath
Va - ter, jetzt fasst er mich an! Erl - kö - nig

seiz'd me with i - cy grasp!" His
hat mir ein Leids ge - than!" Dem

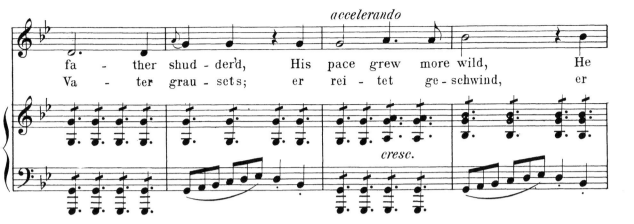

accelerando

fa - ther shud - der'd, His pace grew more wild, He
Va - ter grau - sets; er rei - tet ge - schwind, er

cresc.

held to his bo - som his poor swoon - ing child.
hält in den Ar - men das äch - zen - de Kind.

ff

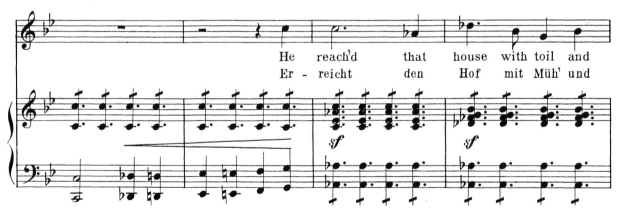

He reach'd that house with toil and
Er - reicht den Hof mit Müh' und

sf *sf*

Recit.

dread, But in his arms, lo! his child lay dead!
Noth: in seinen Ar - men das Kind war todt!

Andante.

fp *pp* *p* *f*

Margaret at the Spinning-wheel.
(GRETCHEN AM SPINNRADE.)

FR. SCHUBERT.

6459

bit - - ter - ness. My poor - - weak head_____ seems
mir_____ ver - gällt. Mein ar - - mer Kopf_____ ist

tem - - pest - toss'd,_____ My poor - - weak sens - - es
mir_____ ver - rückt,_____ mein ar - - mer Sinn_____ ist

seem_____ quite lost. O, my
mir_____ zer - stückt. Mei - ne

heart_____ is sad,_____ my rest_____ is o'er, And
Ruh'_____ ist hin,_____ mein Herz_____ ist schwer, ich

nev - er, a - las!_____ shall I find it, ne'er find_____ it
fin - de, ich fin - de sie nim - mer und nim - - mer -

more.
mehr.

I long ———— my
Mein Bu - sen

arms round him ———— to cast, Could I ———— but
drängt sich nach ——— ihm hin. Ach, dürft' ——— ich

seize him and hold ——— him fast, And kiss, ——— and
fas - sen und hal - ten ihn! und küs - - sen

kiss ——— as I ———— de - sir'd, 'Till on ———— his
ihn, ——— so wie ——— ich wollt', an sei - - nen

kiss - es· my life ———— ex - pir'd. O, could ——— I but
Küs - sen ver - ge - - hen sollt', o' könnt' ——— ich ihn

6458

kiss him as I _____ de - sir'd, 'Till on _____ his
küs - sen, so wie _____ ich wollt', an sei - - nen

kiss - es my life _____ ex - pir'd, 'Till on _____ his
Küs - sen ver - ge - - hen sollt', an sei - - nen

kiss - es my life _____ ex - pir'd.
Küs - sen ver - ge - - hen sollt'!

decresc. e rit.

O, my heart _____ is sad, my
Mei - ne Ruh' _____ ist hin, mein

pp

rest _____ is o'er.
Herz _____ ist schwer!

dim. *ppp*

6459

Hedge-Roses.
(HAIDEN-RÖSLEIN.)

FR. SCHUBERT.

The Wanderer.

(DER WANDERER.)

And ev-er ask while sigh-ing "where?" ev-er "where?" The
und im-mer fragt der Seuf-zer: wo? im-mer wo? Die

sun to me seems dim and cold, The flow'rs are pale, and life seems old; Their
Son-ne dünkt mich hier so kalt, die Blü-the welk, das Le-ben alt, und

speech doth seem but emp-ty sound, And strang-er I on foreign ground.
was sie re-den, lee-rer Schall, ich bin ein Fremdling ü-ber-all.

Poco più mosso.

Where art thou, where art thou, Mine own dear-est land? I
Wo bist du, wo bist du, mein ge-lieb-tes Land? ge-

seek in vain thy far-off
sucht, ge-ahnt, und nie ge-

strand. That land, that land so fresh and green,
kannt! Das Land, das Land so hoff - nungs-grün,

So fresh and green, Where rich - est ros - es
so hoff - nungs-grün, das Land, wo mei - ne

may be seen; Where dwell the friends I love to see, Where sleep the dead so
Ro - sen blüh'n, wo mei - ne Freun - de wandelnd geh'n, wo mei - ne Tod - ten

dear to me, That land where they my lan - guage speak; O land, ___ where
auf - er - steh'n, das Land, das mei - ne Spra - che spricht, o Land, ___ wo

Praise of Tears.

(LOB DER THRÄNEN.)

(A.W. v. Schlegel.)

FR. SCHUBERT.

Andante sostenuto.

PIANO.

Breez - y bow - ers, Per - fum'd
Lau - e Lüf - te, Blu - men -

flow - ers, Days of youth and spring - tide___ blest, Sweet - est
düf - te, al - le Lenz und Ju - gend - lust, fri - scher

kiss - es, Earth - ly bliss - es, Soft - ly lull the ten - der___
Lip - pen Küs - se nip - pen, sanft ge - wiegt an zar - ter___

6462

breast: Wine-cups flow - ing, Nec-tar glow - ing, Dance and
Brust;   dann der Trau - ben Nek-tar rau - ben, Rei - hen-

play   can mirth im - part: Vain af - fec - tion, On re -
tanz   und Spiel und Scherz,   was die Sin - nen nur ge -

sf

flec - tion, Can it fill the thought - ful heart, Can it
win - nen, ach, er - füllt es je das Herz, ach, er -

fill the thought - ful heart?
füllt es je das Herz?

6462

Angel of Beauty.

(SEI MIR GEGRÜSST.)

FR. SCHUBERT.

6439

well,   Dread-ing   fare-well!   In that sweet smile so
küsst,   sei   mir   ge - küsst!   Du von der Hand der

ten-der Truth has plac'd   all his treasure,   Oh!   I feel that I   could sur-
Lie - be die-sem Her - zen ge-geb'-ne,   du   von die-ser Brust   ge-

ren - der My life,   my life with - pleas-ure   To die   with thee,
nomm'ne mir! mit die - sem Thränen-gus - se   sei mir ge - grüsst,

To   die with thee,   To   die   with thee!   Oh! day of
sei mir ge - küsst,   sei mir ge - küsst!   Zum Trotz der

sor - row! Why   should we   sev   -   er.   But tho' a - far to
Fer - ne,   die sich, feind - lich   tren - nend,   hat zwi-schen mich und

mor - row, Think it will not be for__ev - er; Then faith - ful
dich gestellt; dem Neid der Schicksals-mäch - te zum Ver - drus-se sei mir ge-

be, Then faith - ful be, Then faith - ful be!
grüsst, sei mir ge-küsst, sei mir ge - küsst!

Oh! that sweet smil-ing, Free from be-guil-ing
Wie du mir je__ im schön - sten Lenz der Lie - be mit

Bids__ me sub - due__ my poignant grief And hope - ful wait the
Gruss__ und__ Kuss__ ent - ge-gen kamst, mit mei - ner See - le

ad - vent of re - lief. Yes, yes, I see
glü - hendstem Er - gus - se sei mir ge - grüsst,

Faith in Spring.

(FRÜHLINGSGLAUBE.)

FR. SCHUBERT.

row.   New sounds a - rise,   and   o - dors sweet,   And
den.   O fri - scher Duft,   o   neu - er Klang,   o

o - dors sweet,   Oh!   seek, poor heart, the   change   to greet,
neu - er Klang,   nun,   ar - mes Her - ze,   sei   nicht bang!

And cast a - way,   a - way_____ thy sor - row,   And cast a - way thy
nun muss sich al - les,   al - les wen - den,   nun muss sich al - les

cresc.

sor - row.
al-les wen - den.

pp

The earth seems bright - er
Die Welt wird schö - ner mit

ev - 'ry__ morn, While blos - soms__ gay__ her robe__ a - dorn, And
je - dem__ Tag, man weiss nicht, was__ noch wer - den__ mag, das

fair - est flow'rs are bloom - ing, and__ flow'rs are bloom -
Blü - hen will nicht en - den, es__ will nicht en -

ing: They bloom a - round in ev - 'ry vale,
den. Es blüht das__ fern - ste, tief - ste Thal,

They bloom in ev - 'ry vale,
es blüht das tief - ste Thal:

And thou, poor heart, the
Nun, ar - mes Herz, ver-

change must hail,
giss der Qual!

Each day fresh hope, fresh
nun muss sich al - les,

hope___ re-sum - ing,
al - les wen-den,

Each day fresh hope, fresh hope re - sum - ing.
nun muss sich al - les, al - les wen - den.

cresc.   *fp*   *pp*

The Trout.
(DIE FORELLE.)

Poco moderato.　　　　　　　　dimin.　　　　　FR. SCHUBERT.

A stream-let clear and sun — ny With
In ei - nem Bächlein hel - le, da

rip - ples all a - bout, Was once the bath for bon — ny For
schoss in fro - her Eil' die lau - ni - sche Fo - rel - le vor-

gen - tle lit - tle trout. On shore I stood ob - serv — ing With
ü - ber wie ein Pfeil. Ich stand an dem Ge - sta - de und

ex - qui - site de - light. The hap - py lit - tle crea - ture, It
sah in sü - sser Ruh des mun - tern Fischleins Ba - de im

mud - dy And with - out long de - lay. His skil - ful line out-
trü - - be und eh' ich es ge - dacht, so zuck - te sei - ne

reel-ing He caught the fish, the fish so sweet; I
Ru - the, das Fisch - lein, das Fischlein zap-pelt d'ran, und

saw with sadden'd feel - - ing The cheat - ed and the cheat; I
ich mit re - gem Blu - - te sah die Be-trog'ne an, und

saw with sad-den'd feel - - ing The cheat - ed and the cheat.
ich mit re - gem Blu - - te sah die Be-trog'ne an.

The young Nun.

(DIE JUNGE NONNE.)

(Craigher.)

FR. SCHUBERT.

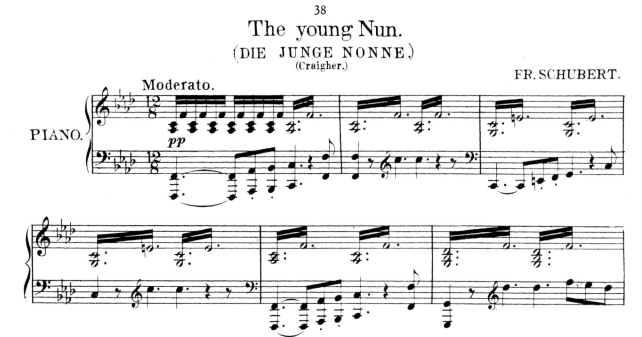

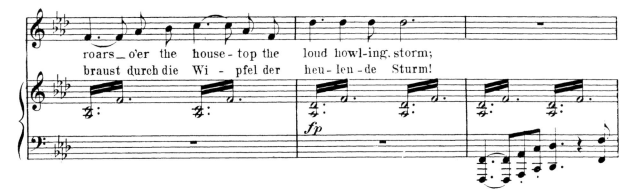

Now
Wie

roars o'er the house-top the loud howl-ing storm;
braust durch die Wi - pfel der heu - len - de Sturm!

And clat - ter the raf - ters, and trem-bles the house;
Es klir - ren die Bal - ken, es zit - tert das Haus!

6171

There roll - eth the thun-der, there
Es rol - let der Don - ner, es

red lightnings flash. The
leuch-tet der Blitz, und

night is all gloom, The night is all
fin - ster die Nacht, und fin - ster die

gloom, Like the
Nacht, wie das

tomb.   Well __ and good,
Grab!   Im - mer-hin,

well __ and good,   E'en so tempest-toss'd   once   was
im - - merhin.   So   tobt' es auch jüngst   noch   in

I !   So   life __ raged within __ me like yon ra - ging storm, So
mir!   Es   braus - te das Le - ben, wie je - tzo der Sturm, es

trem - - tl'd my frame __ like this   frail trem - bling house; __ Love
beb - - ten die Glie - der, wie   je - tzo   das Haus, __ es

flam'd _____ in my heart ___ like yon light - -ning-flash,
flamm - -te die •Lie - be wie je - tzo der Blitz,

cresc.

This soul was all gloom, ___ This
und fin - ster die Ernst, ___ und

p

soul was all gloom, Like ___ the
fin - ster die Brust, wie ___ das

p   *pp*

tomb.   Now
Grab.   Nun

rage — on thy way — thou wild might — y storm, — My
to — be, du wil - der, ge - walt' - - ger Sturm, im

bo — — som is tran-quil, my heart _____ is at rest; — The
Her - - zen ist Frie-de, im Her - - zen ist Ruh'; — des

bride — for the Bride-groom will pa — tient-ly stay, Her
Bräu - ti-gams har - ret die lie - ben-de Braut, ge -

spir - it in cleansing fire is tried, _____ For par — don she
rei - nigt in prü - fen-der Gluth, _____ der e - - wi - gen,

trusts ___ to his in - - fi - nite love. I
e - - wi-gen Lie - - be ge-traut. Ich

wait still Thy com-ing, with yearn - - ing a - bide, ___ Come,
har - re, mein Hei - land! mit seh - - nen - dem Blick! ___ komm,

heav - en - ly Bride - groom, take ___ Thou Thy bride,
himm - li - scher Bräu-ti - gam, ho - - - le die Braut,

Her spir - it set free from her
er - lö - - se die See - le von

pris - on of clay.
ir - discher Haft!
Hark!
Horch,

pp

soft - ly peal - ing from yon - der tow'r sounds the
fried - lich er - tö - net das Glöck - lein vom

bell.
Thurm!
It call's me with sweet-est
Es lockt mich das sü - sse Ge-

tone, And bids me seek in yon - der height E'en
tön all - mäch - tig zu e - wi - gen Höh'n, es

cresc.

Him, who there reigns in pow'r and might, _____ E'en Him, _____ who there
lockt mich das sü - sse Ge - tön _____ all - mäch - tig zu

reigns ev - er in pow - - er and might.
e - - wi-gen, e - - wi-gen Höh'n.

Hal - le - lu - - ja! Hal - le -
Al - le - lu - - ja! Al - le -

lu - - ja!
lu - - ja!

Ave Maria.

(AVE MARIA.)

FR. SCHUBERT.

6538

A - - ve Ma - ri - - - a!
A - - ve Ma - ri - - - a!

Un - - de fil'd! The flint - y_couch whereon we're
Un - - be - fleckt! Wenn wir auf_ die-sen Fels hin-

sleep - ing Shall seem with down of ei - der pil'd, If _
sin - ken zum Schlaf, und uns_ dein Schutz be-deckt, wird

Thou a - bove sweet watch art keep - - ing. The
weich der har - te Fels uns dün - - ken. Du

murk - y cav-ern's air so heav - y Shall breathe of balm if Thou hast
lä - chelst, Ro-sen-düf-te we - hen in die - ser dump-fen Fel-sen-

smil'd; Then, Maid - en, hear a maid-en plead-ing, Oh
kluft; o Mut - ter, hör' des Kin - des Fle-hen, o

Moth - er hear_ a suppliant child! A - ve Ma -
Jung - frau, ei - ne Jung-frau ruft! A - ve Ma -

ri - - a!
ri - - a!

la - den, Now to Thy guidance rec - on - cil'd; Then
beu - gen, da uns dein heil'-ger Trost an - weht; der

hear oh Maid, a sim-ple maid-en, And for a fa - ther hear_ a
Jung - frau wol - le hold dich nei - gen, dem Kind, das für_ den Va - ter

child! A - - ve Ma - ri - -
fleht! A - - ve Ma - ri - -

a!
a!

The Maiden's Lament.
(DES MÄDCHENS KLAGE.)

1. The wild wood rag - es, Dark clouds _ are seen, _ The maid _ sits lone - ly By surg _ es green. The bil - lows are break-ing with
2. My heart is brok - en, And earth _ no more _ My youth's _ fond wish-es Can e'er _ re - store. A - lone up - on Heav-en I
1. Der Eich - wald brau - set, die Wol - ken ziehn, _ das Mägd - lein si - tzet an U - fers Grün, es bricht sich die Wel - le mit
2. „Das Herz ist ge - stor - ben, die Welt _ ist leer, _ und wei - ter giebt sie dem Wun - sche nichts mehr; du Hei - li - ge, ru - fe dein

might,   with might,   And   her   sighs   min - gle   sad ____ With the
call,   I   call,   For   the   joys   of   the   world __ I   have
Macht,   mit Macht, __   und   sie   seufzt hin - aus ____ in die
Kind   zu - rück, __   ich   ha -   be   ge - nos - sen das

gloom __ of __ night; Her   eyes __ with hot tears __ are o'er - flow - ing.
known __ them __ all,   In   lov - ing and be - ing be - lov - ed.
fin - stre __ Nacht,   das   Au - ge vom Wei - nen ge - trü - bet.
ir - di-sche Glück,   ich   ha - be ge - lebt __ und ge - lie - bet."

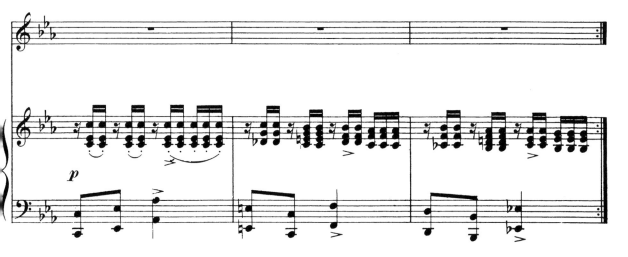

3. My tears are fall - ing, Un - seen __ and vain, __ No
4. The tears are fall - ing, Un - seen __ and vain, __ And
3. Es rin - net der Thrä - nen ver - geb - li-cher Lauf, __ die
4. „Lass rin - nen der Thrä - nen ver - geb - li-cher Lauf, __ es

grief __ can wak - en The dead __ a - gain; Then
grief __ ne'er wak - ens The dead __ a - gain; When
Kla - ge, sie we - cket die Tod - ten nicht auf! Doch
we - cke die Kla - ge den Tod - ten nicht auf! Das

_p_   _cresc._

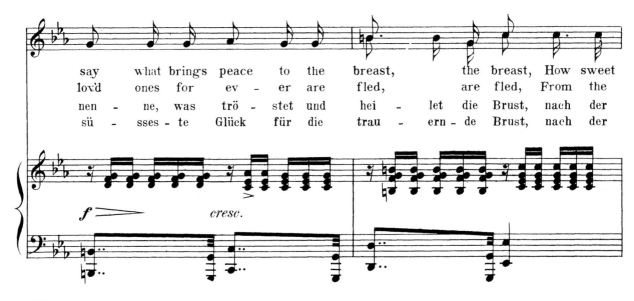

say what brings peace to the breast, the breast, How sweet
lov'd ones for ev - er are fled, are fled, From the
nen - ne, was trö - stet und hei - let die Brust, nach der
sü - sses - te Glück für die trau - ern - de Brust, nach der

_f_   _cresc._

balm may be shed___ from the realms___ of the blest, The
realms___ a - bove___ us a balm ___ may be shed, Like
schö - 'nen Lie _ be ver - schwun - de _ ner Lust; die
schö - nen Lie _ be ver - schwun - de _ ner Lust, sind der

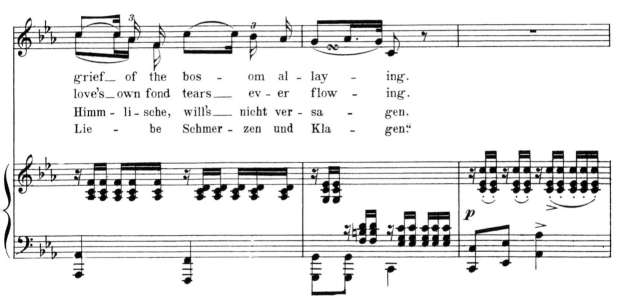

grief___ of the bos - om al - lay - ing.
love's___own fond tears___ ev - er flow - ing.
Himm - li - sche, will's___ nicht ver - sa - gen.
Lie - be Schmer - zen und Kla - gen."

My sweet Repose.

(DU BIST DIE RUH?)

Thou art sweet Peace and tran - quil
Du bist die Ruh, der Frie - de

rest, I long for thee to sooth my breast;
mild, die Sehn - sucht du, und was sie stillt;

I ded - i - cate,___ 'mid_ joys_ and_ sighs, Thy dwell - ing
Ich wei - he dir___ voll_ Lust_ und_ Schmerz, zur Woh - nung

in _____ my _ heart _ and _ eyes, _____ my _ heart _ and _ eyes. _____
hier _____ mein _ Aug' _ und _ Herz, _____ mein _ Aug' _ und _ Herz. _____

Come, then, to me, and close the door, And nev - er,
Kehr' ein bei mir, und schlie - sse du still hin - ter

nev - er leave me more; Chase ev - 'ry pain _____
dir die Pfor - ten zu. Treib' an - dern Schmerz _____

from_ out_ this_ breast, Calm-ing this heart_ to_ joy-ful
aus_ die_-ser Brust, voll sei dies Herz,_ von_ dei-ner_

rest,_ to_joy-ful_ rest.
Lust,_ von_dei-ner_ Lust._

Let thy pure light My
Dies Au-gen-zelt, von

glance con-trol; With lus-tre bright._
dei-nem Glanz al-lein er-hellt,_

Fill thou my soul, ___ Fill thou my soul! ___
o ___ füll' es ___ ganz, ___ o ___ füll' es ___ ganz! ___

Let thy pure light My glance con - trol With
Dies Au - gen - zelt, von dei - nem Glanz al -

lus - tre bright. ___ Fill thou my ___ soul, ___
lein er - hellt, ___ o ___ füll' es ___ ganz, ___

Fill thou my ___ soul! ___
o ___ füll' es ___ ganz! ___

Mignon's Song.
(LIED DER MIGNON.)

FR. SCHUBERT.

Ye who have yearned a-lone My grief can meas-ure, Ye who have yearned a-lone
Nur wer die Sehn-sucht kennt, weiss, was ich lei - de, nur wer die Sehn-sucht kennt,

My grief can meas - ure! No friends are near, and flown Are joy and
weiss, was ich lei - de! Al - lein und ab - ge-trennt von al - ler

pleas-ure. In yon-der sky I see But one di - rec - tion. He's far, who
Freu - de, seh' ich an's Fir-ma-ment nach je - ner Sei - te. Ach! der mich

gave to me His hearts af - fec - tion. I'm
liebt und kennt, ist in der Wei - te. Es

6495

faint, and feel / As though my heart were burn-ing, I'm
schwin-delt mir, / es brennt mein Ein-ge-wei-de, es

cresc.   *f*

faint, and feel / As though my heart were
schwin-delt mir, / es brennt mein Ein-ge-

decresc.   *p*

burn-ing / Ye who have
wei-de. / Nur wer die

decresc.   *pp*

yearned a-lone My grief can meas-ure, Ye who have yearned a-lone
Sehn-sucht kennt, weiss, was ich lei-de, nur wer die Sehn-sucht kennt,

sf

sf

pp

My grief can meas-ure.
weiss, was ich lei-de!

p   *cresc.*   *pp*

6495

To be sung on the Waters.

(Auf dem Wasser zu singen.)

Allegro moderato.

F. SCHUBERT.

Midst the bright sheen of the
Mit - ten im Schimmer der

mir-ror-like wa - ters, Swan - like is float-ing the wa - ver-ingboat;
spie-geln-den Wel - len glei - tet wie Schwä-ne der wan-ken-de Kahn.

Gen-tly__ a - long on those glit-ter-ing wa - ters, Glid-eth our spir-it a-
Ach, auf__ der Freu - de sanft schimmern-den Wel - len glei - tet die See - le da-

way like a boat; Gen-tly_a-long on those glit-ter-ing_wa-ters,
hin wie der Kahn, ach, auf_der_Freu-de sanft schimmern-den_Wel-len

Glid-eth our spir-it a-way like a boat.
glei-tet die See-le da-hin wie der Kahn.

Down from the Heav'ns on the trem-u-lous wa-ters Rich tints of eve-ning il-
Denn von dem Him-mel her-ab auf die Wel-len tan-zet das A-bendroth

lume the swift boat, Rich _____ tints of
rund um den Kahn, tan - - - - zet das

eve-ning il-lume the swift boat.
A-bend-roth rund um den Kahn.

O - ver the beau - ty of each west - ern _ val - ley,
Ü - ber den Wi - pfeln des west - li - chen Hai - nes

Cheer - ful - ly greets us the red - den - ing glow;
win - ket uns freund - lich der röth - li - che Schein.

Un - der _ the branch - es in
Un - ter _ den Zwei - gen des

each east - ern val - ley, Whis - pers the reed in the red - den - ing glow;
öst - li - chen Hai - nes säu - selt der Cal - mus im röth - li - chen Schein;

Un - der _ the branch - es in each east - ern val - ley Whis - pers the reed in the
un - ter _ den Zwei - gen des öst - li - chen Hai - nes säu - selt der Cal - mus im

red‑den‑ing glow.
röth‑li‑chen Schein.

Glad‑ness from heav‑en, and
Freu‑de des Him‑mels und

peace from the val‑ley, Breathe o'er the soul in the red evening glow,
Ru‑he des Hai‑nes ath‑met die Seel' im er‑rö‑thenden Schein,

Breathe _____ o'er the soul in the red eve‑ning
ath ‑ ‑ ‑ ‑ ‑ met die Seel' im er‑rö‑then‑den

glow.
Schein.

5387

Till I, on soar - ing and ra - di - ant pin - ion,
bis ich auf hö - he - rem strah - len - den Flü - gel

Van - ish a - way from the chang - es of time, Van - - -
sel - ber ent - schwin - de der wech - seln - den Zeit, sel - - -

- - - ish a - way from the chang - es of time.
- - - ber ent - schwin - de der wech - seln - den Zeit.

Death and the Maiden.

(DER TOD UND DAS MÄDCHEN.)

FR. SCHUBERT.

Moderato. (♩ = 54.)

PIANO.

pp

The Maiden.
(Das Mädchen.) Poco più moto.

Pass on - ward, Oh! pass on - ward, Wild man with skin - less
Vor - ü - ber, ach, vor - ü - ber, geh' wil - der Kno - chen -

p

bone! I'm but a girl, a - way then, And
mann! Ich bin noch jung, geh' lie - ber! und

leave the young a - lone, And leave the young a - lone.
rüh - re mich nicht an, und rüh - re mich nicht an.

pp dim.

Restless Love.

(RASTLOSE LIEBE.)

(Goethe.)

FR. SCHUBERT.

The fierce storm breast - ing, No mo - ment
Dem Schnee, dem Re - gen, dem Wind ent -

rest - ing, The snow - drift fac - ing, Through dense fog rac - ing,
ge - gen, im Dampf der Klüf - te, durch Ne - bel - düf - te,

Still a - way, still a - way, No
im - mer zu! im - mer zu! oh -

6499

O'er land or sea? All,____ ves, all's____
Wäl - der-wärts zieh'n? Al - - les, al -

cresc.   ff

— un - a - vail - ing.
— les ver - ge - bens.

decresc.   p

Crown of ex - is - tence, bliss - ful an -
Kro - ne des Le - bens, Glück oh - ne

mf   fp   p

noy, Love's rest-less joy, yes, Love's rest-less
Ruh', Lie - be bist du, o Lie - be bist

fp   cresc.

joy. Bliss - ful an-noy____ Love's rest-less joy,____
du. Glück oh - ne Ruh',____ Lie - be bist du,____

p   sf   sf

Crown of ex - is - tence, bliss - ful an - noy,   Love's restless
Kro - ne des Le - bens, Glück oh - ne Ruh',   Lie - be bist

joy, O Love's restless joy, O Love's _____
du, o Lie - be bist du, o Lie - - -

joy,__ Love's restless joy.
be,__ Lie - be bist du.

The Shepherd's Lament.
(SCHÄFERS KLAGELIED.)

6544

Huntman's Even-Song.
(JÄGERS ABENDLIED.)

Molto Andante e piano.

VOICE.

1. I cross the field with stealth - y_ pace, To_
2. thou now pass with win - ning_ grace Thro'
3. feel, when-e'er I_ think on_ thee, As_

VOICE.

1. Im Fel - de schleich' ich still und_ wild, ge-
2. wan - delst jetzt wohl still und_ mild, durch
3. ist es, denk' ich nur an_ dich, als_

Molto Andante e piano.

PIANO.

pp

hunt at e - ven-tide; Thy love-ly form and_ smil-ing face
field . and smil - ing dell? Ah, does my soon-for - got-ten face
if I view'd_ the moon; A calm de-light steals o - ver me,

spannt mein Feu - er-rohr, da schwebt so licht dein lie-bes Bild,
Feld und lie - bes_ Thal, und ach, mein schnell ver - rauschend Bild
in den Mond_____ zu_ seh'n; ein stil-ler Frie - de_ kommt auf mich,

decresc.

1. 2. | **3.**

Be - fore me seem to_glide, Be-fore me seem to glide. 2. Dost
Be - fore thine eye e'er dwell, Be-fore thine eye_ e'er dwell? 3. I
And yet_ my heart's un-done, And yet my heart's un - - done.

dein sü - sses Bild mir vor, dein sü - sses Bild mir vor. 2. Du
stellt sich dir's nicht ein-mal, stellt sich dir's nicht ein-mal? 3. Mir
weiss nicht, wie mir gescheh'n, weiss nicht, wie mir ge - - scheh'n.

1. 2. | **3.**

Wanderer's Nightsong.
(WANDERERS NACHTLIED.)
(Goethe.)

FR. SCHUBERT.

64761

Romance from Rosamund.

(ROSAMUNDE.)

FR. SCHUBERT.

The full moon ris - es— o'er the height, But where, my love,— art—
Der Voll - mond strahlt auf— Ber - ges - höh'n, wie hab' ich dich— ver-

thou?— And where the kiss— of fond de - light That seal'd our— truth - ful
misst!— Du sü - sses Herz! es ist so schön, wenn treu— die— Treu - e—

vow? And where the kiss of fond de - light That— seal'd— our
küsst, du sü - sses Herz! es ist so— schön, wenn— treu— die

truthful vow?
Treu - e— küsst!

In
Was

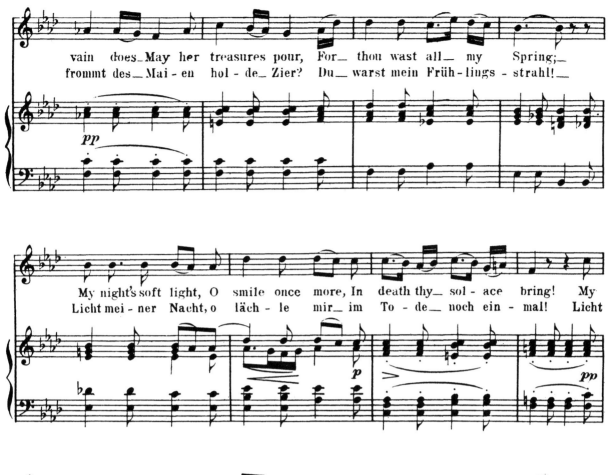

vain does May her treasures pour, For thou wast all my Spring;
fromt des Mai-en hol-de Zier? Du warst mein Früh-lings-strahl!

My night's soft light, O smile once more, In death thy sol-ace bring! My
Licht mei-ner Nacht, o läch-le mir im To-de noch ein-mal! Licht

night's soft light, O smile once more, In death thy sol-ace bring!
mei-ner Nacht, o läch-le mir im To-de noch ein-mal!

With
Sie

heav'n - ward look, re - sign'd and sweet, She stood in the clear moon - shine___ "In
trat hin - ein beim___ Voll - mond-schein, sie blick - te him - mel - wärts:___ „Im

life a - part, in death we meet" She said, "Then al - ways thine!" "In
Le - ben fern, im To - de dein!" und sanft brach Herz an___ Herz. „im

life a - part, in death we___ meet" She___ said,_____ "Then al - ways___ thine!"
Le - ben fern, im To - de___ dein!" und___ sanft_____ brach Herz an___ Herz.

The Secret.

(GEHEIMES.)

Poco Allegro con tenerezza.

PIANO.

At my sweet-hearts ten- der glanc-es
Über mei- nes Lieb-chens Äu-geln

bod- y seems to won- der, I,___ pos-
wun- dert al- le Leu- te, ich,___ der

ses- sor of the se- cret, Know the
Wis- sen- de da- ge- gen, weiss recht

mean- ing hid there- un-der, Know the mean-
gut, was das be- deu-te, weiss recht gut,___

12260

ing hid there un _ _ _ _ der.
_ was das be - deu - _ _ te.

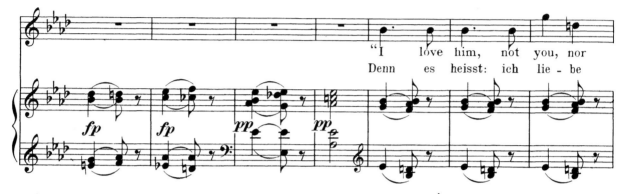

"I love him, not you, nor
Denn es heisst: ich lie - be

you, sir;" This is what those looks be - to - ken;
die - sen, und nicht et - wa den und je - nen,

So, good peo - ple, cease your troub - le, Words could
las - set nur, ihr gu - ten Leu - te, eu - er

not be clear - er_ spo - _ _ ken.
Wun - dern, eu - er_ Seh - _ _ nen.

Yes, when she with pow'r re-sist-less / Flash-es round her
Ja, mit un-ge-heu-ren Mäch-ten / bli-cket sie wohl

joy - ous greet - ing, / To___ him on - ly she dis -
in die Run - de, / doch,_ sie sucht nur zu ver-

cours - - es / Of their next de - light - ful
kün - - den / ihm die näch - ste sü - sse

meet - ing, / Of their next____ de - light - ful__ meet -
Stun - de, / ihm die näch - ste sü - sse__ Stun -

- ing.
- de.

Hark, Hark! the Lark.

(Shakespeare.)

STÄNDCHEN.

FR. SCHUBERT.

hark! the lark at Heav'n's gate sings, And Phoe - bus 'gins___ to

horch, die Lerch' im Ä - ther blau! und Phö - bus, neu___ er-

6504

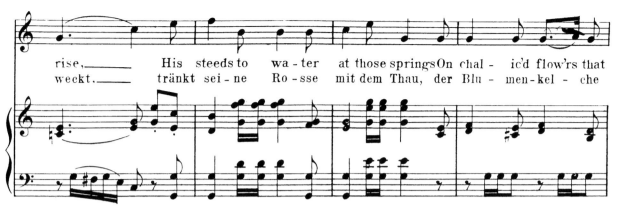

rise,_____ His steeds to wa-ter at those springs On chal - ic'd flow'rs that
weckt._____ tränkt sei-ne Ro-sse mit dem Thau, der Blu-men-kel - che

lies,_____ On chal- ic'd flow'rsthat lies! And wink - ing Ma - ry-
deckt,_____ der Blu-men-kel-che deckt. Der Ring - el-blu - me

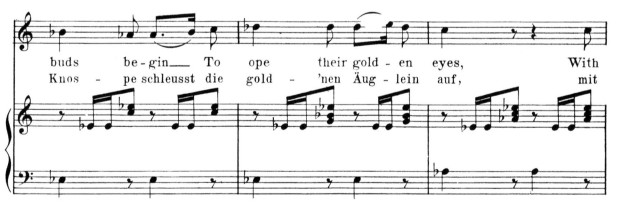

buds be-gin___ To ope their gold-en eyes, With
Knos - pe schleusst die gold - 'nen Äug-lein auf, mit

ev - 'ry-thing that pret - 'y is, My La - dy sweet,__ a-
al - lem, was__ da rei - zend ist__ du sü - sse. Maid,__ steh'

rise, With ev-'ry-thing that pret - ty is, My
auf, mit al - lem was_ da rei - zend ist_ du

La - dy sweet, a - rise,____ a - rise,____ a - rise,____ My
sü - sse Maid,_ steh' auf,____ steh' auf,____ steh' auf,____ du

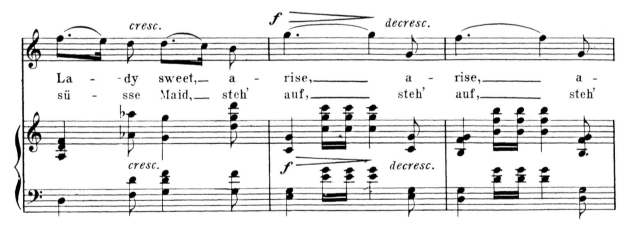

La - dy sweet,_ a - rise,____ a - rise,____ a -
sü - sse Maid,_ steh' auf,____ steh' auf,____ steh'

rise,_____ My La - dy sweet,_ a - rise!
auf,_____ du sü - sse Maid,_ steh' auf!

D. S. al Fine.

6504

Who is Sylvia?

(WAS IST SYLVIA.)

William Shakespeare
From "The Two Gentlemen of Verona"

FR. SCHUBERT.

Moderato.

PIANO.

1. Who is Syl - via, What is she,— That
1. Was ist Syl - via, sa - get an,— dass

all our swains com - mend her? Ho - ly,
sie die wei - te Flur preist? Schön und

fair__ and wise is she;__ The heav'ns such grace did
zart__ seh' ich sie nah'n;__ auf Him - mels Gunst und

lend__ her, That a - dor - ed
Spur__ weis't, dass ihr al - les

6506

she might be,___ That a dored

un ter than,___ dass ihr al les

she might be.

un ter than

2. Is she kind,___ as she is

2. Ist sie schön,___ und gut da-

fair?___ For beau ty lives with kind ness:

zu?___ Reiz labt wie mil de Kind heit;

To her eyes___ love doth re pair,___ To

Ih rem Aug'___ eilt A mor zu,___ dort

help him of his blind - ness; And, be - ing
heilt er sei - ne Blind - heit, und ver -

pp

help'd,— in - hab - its— there,— And, be - ing
weilt— in sü - sser Ruh',— und ver -

help'd, in - hab - its there.
weilt in sü - sser Ruh'.

3. Then to Syl - via
3. Dar - um Syl - via,

pp

let us sing,— That Syl - via is ex - cel - ling,
tön', o Sang,— der hol - den Syl - via Eh - ren,

She ex - cels_ each mor - tal
je - den Reiz_ be - siegt sie

thing_ Up - on the dull earth dwel - ling;
lang,_ den Er - de kann ge - wäh - ren,

To her gar - lands let us_ bring,
Krän - ze_ ihr und Sai - ten - klang,

To her gar - lands let us_ bring.
Krän - ze ihr und Sai - ten - klang.

Farewell.
(ADIEU.)

FR. SCHUBERT.

Andantino espressivo.

PIANO.

Fare-well! our love to sev - er, The part - ing hour is
Schon naht, um uns zu schei - den, der letz - te Au - gen-

near, Thy spir - it soon, for ev - er Will join the heav'n - ly
blick, in's Pa - ra - dies der Freu-den kehr' oh - ne mich zu-

sphere! But thou wilt gain by dy - ing A glo - rious lib - er-
rück! Der Tod kann Frei - heit ge - ben mit mil - der Freun-des-

ty, New flights of rap - ture try - ing, Through all e - ter - ni-
hand, geh' ein zu neu - em Le - ben in je - nes bess' - re

cresc.

65187

well! a mor-row's glad-ness Suc-ceeds a day of pain, And
wohl denn,bis der Mor-gen des neu-en Tags er-scheint, der,

cresc.

hearts that part in sad-ness In heav'n u-nite a-gain. Fare-
fern von Er-den-sor-gen, auf e-wig uns ver-eint. Leb'

p

well! a mor-row's gladness Suc-ceeds a day of pain, And
wohl denn,bis der Mor-gen des neu-en Tags er-scheint, der,

cresc.

hearts that part in sad-ness In heav'n u-nite a-gain.
fern von Er-den-sor-gen, auf e-wig uns ver-eint.

p